GW00854631

The Beatitudes... the blessings from the Sermon on the Mount

By

George Calleja

This book is especially dedicated to all people seeking the Lord.

CONTENTS

Introduction

The book *'The Beatitudes... the blessings from the Sermon on the Mount'* attempts to help the reader grow in his relationship with Jesus.

It presents a brief introduction about the Beatitudes followed by a Chapter dedicated to each Beatitude. Chapter three offers some suggestions as to how the Beatitudes can be lived in our daily lives. It focuses on encouraging every Christian to live the Beatitudes in his daily living, and to be a witness to the people he meets each day.

I hope that you find this book interesting, and that it reaches its aim of helping you in your spiritual growth. May you be blessed through the Beatitudes.

Thank you for reading this book.

George Calleja

Chapter One – The Sermon on the Mount

Ever since the first time I can recall reading the Bible and coming across the Beatitudes as preached by Jesus, better known as the Sermon on the Mount, these particular eight blessings have always been imprinted in my heart. I have always found refuge and encouragement in my life through these blessings … an encouragement that has helped me to increase my faith and trust in the Lord.

I have read this passage many times, especially during difficult moments in my life. On these occasions, I have meditated upon the respective passages, as highlighted in the Gospel of Matthew 5:3-10, I have prayed upon them, and in return I have received His consolation and blessings.

It was not until early 2015, that I felt the need to study these particular verses, and discover their richness in biblical terms. God was showing me that the Beatitudes are filled with spiritual richness, inspired by the Word of Jesus… the Son of God. It was through God's direction that I embarked upon studying these verses. As I went ahead with this study, I felt the need to share this richness with other people, and so God led me to write this book, *'The Beatitudes… the blessings from the Sermon on the Mount'*.

The Sermon on the Mount

In most religions, mountains, maybe because of their altitude and the air of mystery which enshrouds them, are considered to be the point where heaven and earth meet. There are many countries that have their holy mountain where, they claim, the world was created, or where the gods dwell, or the place from where salvation comes *(sourced from the 'Dictionary of Biblical Theology').*

Jesus delivered the *'Sermon on the Mount'* by beginning with the Beatitudes. Traditionally the place of this discourse is located on Karn Hattin (or Kurun Hattîn), that is, the Horns of Hattin, a mountain which receives its name from the little village in Galilee. The *'Dictionary of Biblical Theology'* describes that for Matthew, the mountains of Galilee are the places privileged to witness the manifestations of the Saviour.

The Beatitudes (Matthew 5:3-10)

The term *'beatitude'* comes from the Latin noun *'beātitūdō'* which means *'happiness'*. Each Beatitude consists of two phrases: the condition and the promise. In almost every case the condition is from familiar Old Testament context, but Jesus teaches a new interpretation of such text. Together, the Beatitudes present a new set of Christian ideals that focus on a spirit of love and humility.

This book focuses entirely on the Beatitudes, which are eight blessings as taught by Jesus during the Sermon on the Mount. It is to be pointed out that there are two versions of the Beatitudes which were delivered by Christ during the Sermon on the Mount. One of these versions is from the Gospel of Matthew, while the other is from the Gospel of Luke. As the Beatitudes according to the Gospel of Matthew are the ones that are the most commonly known, this book will focus upon this version. The Beatitudes as indicated in Matthew 5:3-10, are the following:-

Blessed are the poor in spirit,
for theirs is the kingdom of heaven.

Blessed are those who mourn,
for they will be comforted.

Blessed are the meek,
for they will inherit the earth.

Blessed are those who hunger and thirst for righteousness,
for they will be filled.

Blessed are the merciful,
for they will be shown mercy.

Blessed are the pure in heart,
for they will see God.

Blessed are the peacemakers,
for they will be called children of God.

Blessed are those who are persecuted because of righteousness,
for theirs is the kingdom of heaven.

It is a known fact that these eight Beatitudes are the foundation of Christian life. In the *'Modern Catholic Dictionary'* Fr. John A. Hardon, S.J., describes the Beatitudes as the *'promises of happiness made by Christ to those who faithfully accept his teaching and follow his divine example.'*

As described in section 1716 of the *'Catechism of the Catholic Church'* the Beatitudes are at the heart of Jesus' preaching. They take up the promises made to the chosen people since Abraham. The Beatitudes fulfil the promises by ordering them no longer merely to the possession of a territory, but to the Kingdom of heaven.

The Beatitudes are very encouraging. Jesus presented them in a very positive way, focusing on the virtues in life that lead to a reward. The Beatitudes motivate the Christian to love people in different circumstances of life. Love presented through the Beatitudes brings us the promise of salvation. This salvation, which has been a long awaited promise in the Old Testament, is the salvation to the Kingdom of Heaven.

The Beatitudes do not only present the promise of salvation, but also provide peace while facing trials, problems and difficult situations in life while we are still on this earth. According to the contemplation of Saint Gregory of Nyssa, the Beatitudes are:-

"...... a possession of all things held to be good,
from which nothing is absent that a good desire may want.
Perhaps the meaning of beatitude may become clearer to us if it is
compared with its opposite.
Now the opposite of beatitude is misery.
Misery means being afflicted unwillingly with painful sufferings."

Furthermore, in section 1721 of the *'Catechism of the Catholic Church'* it is explained that through the Beatitudes, God put us in the world to know, to love, and to serve him, and so to come to Paradise. The Beatitudes make us *'partakers of the divine nature'* and of eternal life. By living the Beatitudes, man enters into the glory of Christ and into the joy of Trinitarian life. In section 1723 it is further explained that the Beatitude we are promised confronts us with decisive moral choices. It invites us to purify our hearts of bad instincts and to seek the love of God above all else. It teaches us that true happiness is not found in riches or well-being, in human fame or power, or in any human achievement - however beneficial it may be - such as science, technology, and art, or indeed in any creature, but in God alone, the source of every good and of all love.

Chapter Two – The Beatitudes

The First Beatitude

Blessed are the poor in spirit,
for theirs is the kingdom of heaven.

Blessed are the poor in spirit...

Who are the *poor in spirit*? Why is the kingdom of heaven theirs?

The answer behind these two questions rests upon the *spiritual* meaning which Jesus taught during the Sermon on the Mount. The answer is not found through the literal meaning of each word, but in the spiritual, divine meaning relating to a person's response to God's calling. This calling of God to the human being asks of him to recognize his spiritual poverty before going to Him to be able to receive through faith the salvation He offers. This Beatitude asks of the human being to recognize that God is God.

To be poor in spirit is to recognize that you totally depend upon God; to recognize that you are nothing and God is all. To be poor in spirit is to empty oneself, that is, to become nothingness and depend totally on God. So if you happen to be a wealthy person, in a very good financial situation, in the spiritual realm you need to become nothing. You need to recognize and acclaim that although you are a wealthy person, you still depend totally on God. Your attitude should not be that of seeking to be close to God because you are wealthy, but that you grow close to God, because God is God.

On the other hand, if you happen to be a poor person, being in a difficult financial situation, you too need to become nothingness in your particular situation. You need not envy a rich person or desire to become rich. You are to accept your situation of being a poor person, and in that situation you draw close to God, not for the sake of seeking comfort from God, but because God is God.

This is the way to be poor in spirit: to become nothing, knowing that you totally depend upon God. The person who is poor in spirit, recognizes his smallness in front of God, and recognizes that God is everything in his life.

This is a challenge in today's life as every day the Christian's spirituality is bombarded by worldly ideas through the different social media. In the midst of all these voices, we are to recognize that we totally depend on God; we are to empty ourselves and let God penetrate our heart.

...for theirs is the kingdom of heaven.

Isn't it great that people are blessed because they choose to be poor in spirit? The result of being blessed is that the kingdom of heaven is theirs. So, what is the kingdom of heaven?

The kingdom of heaven is the gift of salvation. It is the gift for all who are poor in spirit. This gift was brought to us by the loving act of Jesus… that of dying on the cross for our sins. It is precisely in front of the cross that people are to recognize their sins, to recognize that Christ is the saviour who redeemed us from our sins. It is Jesus on the cross that made it possible for us to be redeemed from our sins. We must increase our faith in what Jesus did for us through his death on the cross.

Upon recognizing our sins, our weaknesses, recognizing that Christ is the saviour... the gift of salvation is ours. It is at this point in our faith that the kingdom of heaven already becomes ours, even as from here on earth.

The Second Beatitude

Blessed are those who mourn,
for they will be comforted.

Blessed are those who mourn...

Who are those who mourn? Why will they be comforted?

'Those who mourn' refers to those people who are spiritually sorrowful. These are the people who grieve over their own sins, who grieve over the sins of others. These people have realised their sin, have understood their mistakes, have asked for forgiveness. These people might be still bearing the consequence of sin, maybe because they are in prison, or separated from their families, or without a job; but despite this situation, they yearn for the joys and peace of heaven.

People who have been released from sin are glad to have been saved by Him, that is, to have received the salvation from Jesus. They mourn for they do not want to fall back to sin, but they want to continue living in the path of His salvation. These people have realised that there is no fulfilment when living in sin….

These people are humble, they fully recognise His salvation over sin, but still have to live in this world bearing the consequence of sin, knowing, however, that the consequence of their sin will not be eternal, as in heaven there is only joy and peace through being in the presence of the Father, the Son and Holy Spirit.

Where do you stand in your life… are you spiritually sorrowful? Do you grieve over your sins? Have you recognised His salvation over your sins?

…for they will be comforted.

People who recognise their sins, and mourn over them, will be comforted by Him… comforted in a personal way by Jesus. This is the gift from Him for whoever mourns over his sins… to receive the comfort from Jesus, the comfort of a loving merciful Father. The loving Father always opens His arms to receive a redeemed person and welcomes him back to be comforted.

This comfort is the result of the Father welcoming back the lost sheep, welcoming back the person who was astray in sin, who deserted the family and friends, who was living a life of sin. The Father's comfort will give the fallen person the joy and peace of salvation, and at the same time gives the person the strength to bear the consequence of his sin on earth.

The comfort received by the person, will give him the strength not to look back in life, but to look forward. This comfort will help the person to live each present moment by loving the neighbour, doing acts of love by being Jesus to others. This spiritual comfort from the Father will embrace the person and will give him the spiritual strength he needs to grow in his faith, to stay on the road to follow Jesus, and to be a witness to others of His love and comfort.

The Third Beatitude

Blessed are the meek,
for they will inherit the earth.

Blessed are the meek...

Who are the meek? Why will they inherit the earth?

A dictionary term for the word *'meek'* describes those people who are quiet and gentle in nature, and reluctant to fight or argue with other people. These people, in today's society, are difficult to find.

From a Christian perspective and through the teachings of Jesus, the meek are those who bear patiently all the contradictions of life, accepting these situations as happening through God's Will or by His permission. In addition to this, the meek are people who have peace of heart and also peace of life, in spite of the difficult times in their lives. These people, who live their lives by accepting God's Will, are people who are loved and respected.

People who live meekness through the grace of God are also able to take control of their anger. Their spiritual experience of God helps them to master impatience and also to control any desires leading to seeking revenge of another person.

A meek person is one who is Jesus to others, loving the people he meets each moment of his life. Living meekness is possible when we embrace His will for our lives.

...for they will inherit the earth.

Because a meek person, from a spiritual perspective, does not get angry or seek revenge, the result is that they will inherit the earth. A meek person inherits the earth because instead of hurting another person over a particular situation, such as an argument, being hurt etc… a meek person seeks to forgive the other person… he forgives his enemies… he does what Jesus would have done: he chooses to keep loving.

Furthermore, a meek person does not only forgive the other person, but goes a step further… he seeks to win back the other person and bring him to Christ. This is a meek person: he is interested in his neighbour, forgiving him and drawing him closer to Christ. A meek person will do his utmost to help his neighbour get to know that Christ loves him in a personal way.

For the above actions, the meek person will inherit the earth. How many times in your life have you acted as a meek person? How many times have you helped your neighbour to draw closer to Christ? It is through being a meek person that you will inherit the earth.

The Fourth Beatitude

Blessed are those who hunger and thirst for righteousness, for they will be filled.

Blessed are those who hunger and thirst for righteousness…

Have you ever experienced wanting to know more about God? Have you ever cried out to God about wanting to know Him in a personal way? Those who foster inside them the desire of knowing God, of giving themselves to Him and growing in their spiritual life, desiring to be filled by the gifts of the Holy Spirit… are the people who yearn for righteousness to be lived in the world. This is so true, as only

God is righteous. The Father, Son and Holy Spirit are one in perfection, and they radiate righteousness to the world.

In this context, to be *'hungry'* for God is the eagerness for spiritual growth of a person. That is, the desire to be Jesus for others by being in harmony with the peace of the Holy Trinity. This eagerness of the individual to become a better person is tested by carrying out acts of love with his neighbour. One also becomes more humble and pure in spirit and in the mind… this results from becoming more closely united with God.

…for they will be filled.

Becoming a more humble and pure person, which leads to being closer to God, means becoming a holier person. This person grows in purity and in sanctity. This is possible by participating, through the Holy Spirit, in Divine holiness. Being filled with holiness is the result of cutting one self off from sin.

To be a holy person is not beyond the possibilities of anyone… it only takes to love God and to love one's neighbour. Holiness is for everyone. It is the way to be close to God.

The Fifth Beatitude

Blessed are the merciful,
for they will be shown mercy.

Blessed are the merciful...

A merciful person is a person who does God's will in response to His love. Jesus showed His kindness, compassion, respect and tenderness to all people... He gave each person the love of the Father. In this same way, a person who in his life follows Jesus and does His will is a person who is merciful to his neighbour.

A merciful person is one who, out of his spiritual relationship with Jesus, performs acts of love, by feeding the hungry, giving to drink to the thirsty, sheltering the homeless, visiting the sick and visiting the imprisoned. Furthermore, a merciful person, amongst others, also teaches the ignorant, counsels the doubtful, forgives offences and comforts the afflicted.

A merciful person sees life not just from a human perspective; he sees life through the eyes of Jesus. By being merciful, such a person approaches each day by living experiences and relationships with others with the aim of giving them Christ.

To be merciful is a challenge for us. How many times in our lives have we met a hungry or thirsty person, a homeless person...? Have we been merciful to them? Have we given them to eat and drink? If we were hungry and thirsty or homeless ourselves, would we not want someone to give us to eat, to drink and to provide us with shelter?

We are to be a merciful people.

...for they will be shown mercy.

Acting in a merciful way will bring joy, peace and hope to those receiving these merciful acts of love. Furthermore, the merciful person will himself be shown mercy. When judgement day will come for these merciful persons, as it is written in Matthew 25:34-36, Christ will say to them:

> ..... *'Come, you who are blessed by my Father; take your inheritance, the kingdom prepared for you since the creation of the world. For I was hungry and you gave me something to eat, I was thirsty and you gave me something to drink, I was a stranger and you invited me in, I needed clothes and you clothed me, I was sick and you looked after me, I was in prison and you came to visit me.'*

This is what Jesus will show to merciful persons… the Kingdom of Heaven. Be a merciful person and the Kingdom of heaven is yours.

The Sixth Beatitude

Blessed are the pure in heart,
for they will see God.

Blessed are the pure in heart...

What does this particular Beatitude show us about Jesus' love for us? This Beatitude shows us the _'depth'_ of Jesus' love for us by being interested in our heart. What is important for Jesus is not the many good deeds that we do, but he is interested in knowing that such good deeds are done with a pure, clean heart.

Jesus is interested in sinners being able to make it to the loving Father, by acknowledging their mistakes, by asking forgiveness and by changing their lives. This is only possible if each sinner changes his life of sin that results in an unclean heart, and through the love of the Father be transformed to have a clean, pure heart that disassociates itself from sin.

The heart carries all the secrets of a person, which only the person himself knows about... besides God. Amongst such secrets, one may carry negative secrets, which as is written in Matthew 15-18-20 the _'...things that come out of a person's mouth come from the heart, and these defile them. For out of the heart come evil thoughts - murder, adultery, sexual immorality, theft, false testimony, slander. These are what defile a person...'_

It is for this reason that Jesus is very much interested in our heart, in having a pure heart, so that mankind does not fall into the trap of sin. This particular Beatitude gives the person hope to trust in Him by letting go of sin and as a result obtain a clean heart.

...for they will see God.

The reward for all those who are clean in heart and who renounce sin from their lives is, to see God. What ultimate reward can anyone hope for in one's life, other than that of seeing God?

This is Jesus' ultimate love for us all: teaching us how to become a better person to overcome sin and reap the reward through a pure heart. The reward of seeing God is there for all of us to achieve by experiencing the love of God given to us on earth, and by seeing God in heaven... which is the greatest reward for eternity.

It is only through Him that we can be purified. Are you working to have a clean and pure heart? What obstacles are there in your life preventing you from having a clean heart? Through God's grace, through His love for you, it is possible for you to have a clean heart and to be rewarded for it by seeing God.

God is waiting for you.

The Seventh Beatitude

Blessed are the peacemakers,
for they will be called children of God.

Blessed are the peacemakers...

How many times in our lives have we wished that there be peace in the world! This seventh Beatitude addresses those people who not only try to live in peace in their personal life, but who also work and take initiatives to bring peace to the world. Jesus referred to these people as blessed, because through their actions and deeds they work for and promote peace.

These persons are interested in loving other people around them, to bring peace to them even when there is some kind of trouble or misunderstanding of some sort. Where there is no peace, these people who Jesus called blessed, do their utmost to restore peace wherever they are.

The world yearns to have more people like these… genuine peacemakers who take an interest in those around them, by loving them as Jesus loves them. What loving actions have you undertaken in your life to be a peacemaker, the way that Jesus wants you to be?

...for they will be called children of God.

God considers these people who work for peace, as children of heaven. These people are dearly loved by God. It is for these reasons

that Jesus emphasized… *'that they will be called children of God'.*
The end result for the people who work for peace is that they will be
considered as children of God. Do you want to be a child of God?

It is really worth working for peace and experiencing the result of
reconciliation in this world. It is very important that as Christians we
feel encouraged to go out and be peacemakers through the love of
God. All this leads to being called a child of God.

The world is waiting for you to be a true peacemaker.

The Eighth Beatitude

***Blessed are those who are persecuted because of righteousness,
for theirs is the kingdom of heaven.***

Blessed are those who are persecuted because of righteousness…

On numerous occasions, we have heard stories about Christians who
have been persecuted for being witnesses to God's love. Today,
through all kind of social media we hear of Christians' sufferings for
defending their faith, the Church, Christian values, or for working
for peace on earth.

The eighth Beatitude speaks precisely about this: that all those who
in their lives are persecuted for living up to the truth, will be blessed
for being righteous. It is a reality that keeps happening around us,
that Christians are persecuted and face different sufferings for being

faithful to the truth. Jesus knows this kind of suffering will continue to take place till the very end of time, but He also knows that through the love and unity of the Holy Trinity, these same people who experience these sufferings… will be blessed.

Do you recall any episode in your life when you have been persecuted because of your faith? What was your experience of it? Or maybe, have you never been persecuted, because you have never been a real witness to your faith? Does this make you wonder if you are truly living up to your faith?

…for theirs is the kingdom of heaven.

The blessing that Jesus preached in this Beatitude is that people who face persecution and suffering for their faith… will receive the kingdom of heaven as their own. This is the reward for these people… for all those who suffer persecution… they will receive the eternal reward of the kingdom of heaven.

Being blessed by receiving the kingdom of heaven is possible whenever the faith of the individual penetrates the mystery of being persecuted, that is, whenever one finds his hope in the faith in God. Through the strong faith in God, one suffers persecution with joy… knowing that his reward is the kingdom of God *(sourced from the 'Dictionary of Biblical Theology').*

Oh, how much I really want to receive the kingdom of heaven! The truth is that this opportunity is there for all… for me, for you, for all people who have a deep faith in God… our loving Father.

Chapter Three – Living the Beatitudes

A person who fully lives the Beatitudes, is a person who does God's will in every moment of his life. This is a person that pleases God and brings hope and love to humanity. This is a person that today's society needs and thirsts for... to be the messenger of God's love in today's world... in today's culture.

But, in this *'modern'* world of ours, a world that has changed and developed over time since Jesus preached the Beatitudes, how is it possible to live such Beatitudes? Are the Beatitudes preached by Jesus still relevant in today's life? What must one do to truly live them to the full and be rewarded with the different blessings?

An intimate relationship with the Holy Trinity
To live the Beatitudes and experience them in your life requires an intimate relationship with the Holy Trinity... that is, a personal relationship with the Father, the Son and the Holy Spirit. This relationship is the result of a process of a Christian's spiritual growth. This process is only possible if one sincerely desires to have a personal relationship with the Holy Spirit, casting sin out of his life, seeking God's presence through the Eucharist and/or through the Word of God, and seeking to be another Jesus to one's neighbour.

The Holy Spirit gives the person His special grace by enlightening him to better understand the Word of God, by giving him the courage to go out and proclaim the Good News, by showing him the way to follow Jesus. This relationship with the Holy Spirit will make that person stronger in his faith and more courageous to be a witness to God's love.

Knowing the Word of God

Knowing the Word of God, that is, knowing the true meaning of what is written in the Bible is another way to help one to live the Beatitudes. The Word of God will help the individual to understand better the meaning behind each Beatitude, how to live it and practice it each day. To know the Word of God it is important to find good quality time to read it, to pray upon it and to listen to God through the Holy Scriptures.

The Word of God lived in one's life will give him the strength to go against the current of a society not believing in God... to be the one who brings peace and love around him.

Go... and love your neighbour

As seen earlier in this book, the Beatitudes are based on loving your neighbour. Being Jesus to others is what a true Christian should be, and this is achieved by '*dying*' for others. As I have already mentioned in one of my previous books titled '*Yes... I Will Follow Him*', "...*we are to preach the gospel to all creation. So all creation is our neighbour... Our neighbour is the person we meet during our daily encounters. And He has called us to evangelize our neighbour to believe and be baptized... only through His name... and He will protect us."*

This is a challenge we are to seriously take up in our lives: to spread the Good News to our neighbours. Unless we do so, we cannot expect to be blessed, as is mentioned in the Beatitudes. We will be missing it all... we will not see the Kingdom of God.

To be blessed as promised in the Beatitudes, we are to love our neighbour. Loving our neighbour is possible the more we live in a special relationship with the Holy Spirit. It is then that we can experience a flow of joy, of love, and happiness. When we love our neighbour, God will bless us with His Kingdom and the other blessings as mentioned in each of the Beatitudes.

The blessings of the Beatitudes

The Beatitudes present a new set of Christian ideals that focus on a spirit of love and humility. This is what this book has tried to bring to you... that you too may have this spirit of love and humility.

The blessings of the Beatitudes are there for us all to experience in our present life and after. It is possible to love our neighbour, to be a witness of His love. This is possible if we totally give our lives to

Him and let Him take total control of our mind, our soul and our spirit.

This is the decision that I and you, have to take… that of being Jesus to others. The blessings of the Beatitudes are there… for me, for you… if we live our life through the love and will of God.

Remember… these blessings are there for you too, to discover and live!

Blessed are the poor in spirit,
for theirs is the kingdom of heaven.

Blessed are those who mourn,
for they will be comforted.

Blessed are the meek,
for they will inherit the earth.

Blessed are those who hunger and thirst for righteousness,
for they will be filled.

Blessed are the merciful,
for they will be shown mercy.

Blessed are the pure in heart,
for they will see God.

Blessed are the peacemakers,
for they will be called children of God.

Blessed are those who are persecuted because of righteousness,
for theirs is the kingdom of heaven.

About the Author

I am George Calleja from Malta; I am married and have two children. In 2009 I obtained my MBA through the University of Leicester.

During the years 1990 to 1996 I was a full time missionary with *'The International Catholic Programme for Evangelization - ICPE'* and have evangelized in various countries, such as Russia, Ghana, Poland, Germany, and Malta amongst others. Since 1997, I am an active member of the Focolare Movement in Malta.

My first ebook *'Peace and Unity in our lives – Volume One'* was published in November 2014. In January 2015, I published my second ebook, which is *Volume Two* of *Peace and Unity in our lives'*. This was followed by my third ebook *'Yes... I will follow Him'*, published in March 2015, which is also available in paperback. During this month, I also published the paperback version of *'Peace and Unity in our lives'*. In June 2015 I published my fourth ebook *'Evangelization through Social Networking Sites'* which is free to download.

Through my books and various other writings available through my social networks and also as a contributor to Catholic.365, I try to share my thoughts based on my spiritual experience, with whoever is seeking to appreciate life... Ultimately, I hope that the reader will become closer in his relationship with Jesus.

I hope that you enjoy my writings and above all, that you find spiritual growth through them.

Connect with the Author

If you would like to contact me, please email me at:

peacethroughunity@gmail.com

You can also follow me through the following links:-

Blog: *http://peacethroughunity.blogspot.com/*

FaceBook:

https://www.facebook.com/georgecallejaebooks/timeline

GoodReads: *https://www.goodreads.com/user/show/41803402-*

george-calleja

Google+:

https://plus.google.com/u/0/114381802793936205378/posts

Twitter: *https://twitter.com/PeaceUnityLives*

Website: *https://sites.google.com/site/peaceinunity/*

WordPress: *http://peacethroughunity.wordpress.com/*

Future books to be published

By the end of December 2015 I am planning to publish my sixth book, *'My little book of daily prayer'*. Most of the writing of this book is already completed. The aim of this book is to provide a daily short prayer, which is accompanied by a short reflection for each month of the year. This book is recommended for people who are still in their beginning of their walk with Jesus, and also for those who have deepened their faith in God, but would like an easy book of prayer to refer to during the day.

I am planning other books to be published, with the aim of reaching the people's heart to get closer to Jesus. With this in view, I am constantly planning and writing basic notes for my future books!

For further information about my publications, please visit my profile on FaceBook at:
https://www.facebook.com/georgecallejaebooks/timeline
or visit my website 'George Calleja – Christian author' at:
https://sites.google.com/site/georgecallejachristianauthor/

Published books

'Evangelization through Social Networking Sites'

Published: 14 June 2015

Words: 6,860

Language: English

Religion and Spirituality: Christian Life / General

ISBN: 9781310647598

'Yes... I will follow Him'

Published: 8 March 2015

Words: 9,020

Language: English

Religion and Spirituality: Christian Life / General

ISBN: 1507818939

Reviewed by: Robert A. Hunt

https://www.facebook.com/profile.php?id=100007192625193

'I have thoroughly enjoyed reading this book. I strongly recommend anyone to read "Yes I Will Follow Him" by George Calleja. It was beautifully written. I admire how George Calleja let go of his job and family and did ministry for 6 years abroad. It is not easy to let go of everything and just follow Jesus. But there is so much more

reward and blessing in following Jesus. I really enjoyed the different verses George mentioned like when Mary was visited by the angel and was told that she would give birth to Jesus, God's son and how she just said yes to the lord, trusting him completely. There is so much for a reader to learn in this novel and I would recommend this to anyone who is interested in exploring a closer relationship with the Lord.'

<u>Reviewed by:</u> Joshua Linden http://www.joshuaklinden.com/

'When it comes to religious/spiritual themes I prefer shorter books such as The Tao or The Cloud of Unknowing. Like these books Calleja gives the reader a singular concept upon which to meditate—the concept of saying "yes" to Jesus. A wise teacher of mine once said, "There is room in love to say 'no'". For most of us there are many to who "no" is the appropriate response. In 'Yes'...I will follow Him, Calleja presents a simple truth—that saying "yes" to Jesus loses one nothing and gains one everything. A very delightful meditation on love.'

'Peace and Unity in our lives – Volume Two'

Published: 21 January 2015

Words: 8,160

Language: English

Religion and Spirituality: Christian Life / General

ISBN: 9781310758577

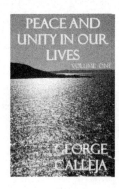

'Peace and Unity in our lives – Volume One'

Published: 9 November 2014

Words: 6,300

Language: English

Religion and Spirituality: Christian Life / General

ISBN: 9781310773280

While thanking you for having the time to read this book, I hope that it helped you to increase your faith. I appreciate that you write a review about reading this book on the site from where you bought it.

Printed in Great Britain
by Amazon